Helena the Fighter

INTRO TO PHASE 5

/u_e/

Level 4+
Blue+

BookLife Readers

Helpful Hints for Reading at Home

The graphemes (written letters) and phonemes (units of sound) used throughout this series are aligned with Letters and Sounds. This offers a consistent approach to learning whether reading at home or in the classroom.

THIS BLUE+ BOOK BAND SERVES AS AN INTRODUCTION TO PHASE 5. EACH BOOK IN THIS BAND USES ALL PHONEMES LEARNED UP TO PHASE 4, WHILE INTRODUCING ONE PHASE 5 PHONEME. HERE IS A LIST OF PHONEMES FOR THIS PHASE, WITH THE NEW PHASE 5 PHONEME. AN EXAMPLE OF THE PRONUNCIATION CAN BE FOUND IN BRACKETS.

Phase 3			
j (jug)	v (van)	w (wet)	x (fox)
y (yellow)	z (zoo)	zz (buzz)	qu (quick)
ch (chip)	sh (shop)	th (thin/then)	ng (ring)
ai (rain)	ee (feet)	igh (night)	oa (boat)
oo (boot/look)	ar (farm)	or (for)	ur (hurt)
ow (cow)	oi (coin)	ear (dear)	air (fair)
ure (sure)	er (corner)		

New Phase 5 Phoneme	
u_e (use, fortune, refuse)	

HERE ARE SOME WORDS WHICH YOUR CHILD MAY FIND TRICKY.

Phase 4 Tricky Words			
said	were	have	there
like	little	so	one
do	when	some	out
come	what		

TOP TIPS FOR HELPING YOUR CHILD TO READ:

- Allow children time to break down unfamiliar words into units of sound and then encourage children to string these sounds together to create the word.

- Encourage your child to point out any focus phonics when they are used.

- Read through the book more than once to grow confidence.

- Ask simple questions about the text to assess understanding.

- Encourage children to use illustrations as prompts.

INTRO TO PHASE 5 /u_e/

This book introduces the phoneme /u_e/ and is a Blue+ Level 4+ book band.

Helena the Fighter

Written by
Madeline Tyler

Illustrated by
Marianne Constable

Helena is from a land of fighters. She thinks that she is the best fighter ever.

Her dad is the king of all the land, but he is not a fair king.

He gets all the cash and coins and keeps it all for himself. He is selfish.

"You can use this fortune to help the crowds," Helena tells him.
"I refuse," he grunts.

"This is boring," the king tells the queen one morning. "Amuse me!"

Helena is clever. She has a plan to amuse the king and help the crowds.

"A contest!" Helena tells him. "The fighter that gets to the end wins the fortune!"

"Alex the Colossus will fight for me. I refuse not to win," he tells her.

"I will fight for the crowds," yells Helena.
"No, Helena, you are far too cute."

Helena is not cute at all. She gets her costume and her bag. She will fight.

The contest begins with a dog. "We will not attack a cute dog!" yells a fighter.

But then the dog growls. Some fighters run, but the dog is too quick. Chomp!

Helena has a plan. She chucks the dog a cube of food.

Helena pats the dog and runs to the next part of the contest.

The fighters are afraid.
"I wish I was back with that dog," one of them mutters.

One of the fighters cuts the monster, but that is not the right thing to do.

I can confuse it, Helena thinks. She lights a fuse and waits.

Bang! Boom! The monster looks up.
Helena and Alex can get across.

It is the end of the contest, and it is just Helena and Alex now.

She needs to be clever to win the fortune. She thinks long and hard.

Helena creeps up to the monster and hums a tune.

She jumps on the sleeping monster and gets to the end.

Helena rips off her costume and the king is mute. He is in shock.

"I am the winner. You must hand the fortune to the crowds," Helena yells.

"Excuse me..." the king fumes. But the queen nods, and hands back the fortune.

The king is mad, but he cannot fight back. Helena is the best fighter ever.

Helena the Fighter

1) What does Helena think she is the best at?

2) What was the first monster in the contest?
   a) Dragon
   b) Goblin
   c) Three-headed dog

3) How does Helena get past the sea monster?

4) What would you do with the fortune if you won the contest?

5) The king doesn't believe in Helena, but she proves him wrong. Have you ever proved someone wrong?

BookLife PUBLISHING

BookLife Readers

©2022 **BookLife Publishing Ltd.**
King's Lynn, Norfolk PE30 4LS

ISBN 978-1-80155-066-6

All rights reserved. Printed in Poland.
A catalogue record for this book is available from the British Library.

Helena the Fighter
Written by Madeline Tyler
Illustrated by Marianne Constable

An Introduction to BookLife Readers...

Our Readers have been specifically created in line with the London Institute of Education's approach to book banding and are phonetically decodable and ordered to support each phase of the Letters and Sounds document.

Each book has been created to provide the best possible reading and learning experience. Our aim is to share our love of books with children, providing both emerging readers and prolific page-turners with beautiful books that are guaranteed to provoke interest and learning, regardless of ability.

BOOK BAND GRADED using the Institute of Education's approach to levelling.

PHONETICALLY DECODABLE supporting each phase of Letters and Sounds.

EXERCISES AND QUESTIONS to offer reinforcement and to ascertain comprehension.

BEAUTIFULLY ILLUSTRATED to inspire and provoke engagement, providing a variety of styles for the reader to enjoy whilst reading through the series.

AUTHOR INSIGHT: MADELINE TYLER

Native to Norfolk, England, Madeline Tyler's intelligence and professionalism can be felt in the 50-plus books that she has written for BookLife Publishing. A graduate of Queen Mary University of London with a 1st Class degree in Comparative Literature, she also received a University Volunteering Award for helping children to read at a local school.

When she was a child, Madeline enjoyed playing the violin, and she now relaxes through yoga and reading books!

INTRO TO PHASE 5 /u_e/

This book introduces the phoneme /u_e/ and is a Blue+ Level 4+ book band.